Visible mending: Everyday repairs in the South West

Steven Bond, Caitlin DeSilvey & James R. Ryan

Visible mending
Everyday repairs in the South West

Uniformbooks 2013

The original 'Small is Beautiful?' project was funded by the Arts and Humanities Research Council (grant number AH/H038914/1) and made possible by the makers and menders who shared the journey with us. Thank you.

This book is dedicated to Jenny, and to Peter, whose knowledge, skills and generosity helped inspire this project, and, no doubt, countless others.

First published 2013
Edited and designed by Colin Sackett and Steven Bond
Copyright © Images: Steven Bond/University of Exeter;
Text: Caitlin DeSilvey, James R. Ryan
ISBN 978-0-9568559-9-2

Published as part of the Centre for Environmental Arts and Humanities/Uniformbooks series. The Centre, which is based at the University of Exeter's Penryn Campus, creates opportunities for shared investigation of the complex relationship between the environment and the human imagination. The series focuses on the publication of intellectually accessible, creatively conceived and conceptually provocative short volumes, relevant to both academic and public audiences.

Uniformbooks
7 Hillhead Terrace, Axminster, Devon EX13 5JL
www.uniformbooks.co.uk

Printed and bound by R. Booth Ltd, Penryn, Cornwall

Contents

....

Nick Hand

....

Foreword

Like makers, the repairers of beautiful and functional objects have an honesty and integrity that is wholly inspiring. If you spend time in any of their workshops you will be in awe of their great knowledge and skill and you will leave with a happy heart.

This project has been put together with love and care. I know that Steven, Caitlin and James have been inspired in much the same way as I have in meeting and recording these people and their work-shops. The elegant design of the book itself—its simple, functional style—brings the character of people and places alive; even echoing the images of the repairer's neatly ordered drawers.

The wonderful images show the patina of years of working on a bench, the tools worn smooth by continuous use, the gentle detail of the workspaces. You can almost smell the inks and oils that surround them. And the hands of the repairers themselves reflect their work, sometimes engrained skin and chipped nails, sometimes the long elegant fingers of an artist.

As well as recording these artisans, their skills and their work-places, the book acts as a reminder that we need to support the repairers; to keep their skills alive, to repair rather than to replace. Their skills need to be passed on to future generations so that our treasured possessions—and our everyday things—stay in fine working order.

Nick Hand is a graphic designer, photographer and cyclist. He has spent much of the past four years making photofilms of craftsmen and women mostly in the UK, but also in America and Italy. His book *Conversations on the Coast* follows his journey by bicycle around the coast of Britain and Ireland recording the lives of artisans that he met along the way. He is currently producing a similar book about a journey along the Hudson Valley in New York.

Sarah Pink

Prologue: repairing as making

Repairing takes many different forms. It is not always about the mending of material objects, and it is not always even noticeable. It is something that we do in an ongoing way, and it is often not remarked on or recognised. Repairing can be thought of as the work of the maker, who, as the anthropologist Tim Ingold tells us, differs from the designer. Making, according to Ingold, is to do with the "capacity to find the grain of the world's becoming and bend it to its evolving purpose". If, as he proposes, "the maker… is a master of improvisation, of making do with whatever is at hand",[1] then the mender is she or he who brings together what is needed to re-make whatever is at hand. Indeed we might ask what, if any, is the difference between the mender and the maker. If we see making as an ongoing process, in which multiple people potentially participate during the biography of an object or thing, then it is never a definitively completed act. It is indeed the way that things are mended and melded by their subsequent human carers that defines their status as emergent, as changing objects or processes. They are never restored to what they were before, but are remade to emerge as something else, and to enter the future. Yet these changes, these remakings (rather than restorings) often fall below the horizon of the human eye, and are sometimes so mundane that they are not even spoken about.

Repair, mending and making also often involve the knowing touch of the skilled hand, being able—by looking at or sensing something —to know what needs to be done, and to know when it feels right. These skills are part of tacit and unspoken ways of knowing, and are learned by doing, not usually verbalized. Photography, then, is an ideal way to express what it means to repair, mend and make. Many of the photographs in this book are close-up. They take us right to the surfaces and forms of objects that have been repaired, and show us the marks on them that, if they could speak, would narrate their stories.

Yet photographs are not static, and neither do they freeze the objects featured in them. Photographs catch a moment, and as the photographer goes through the world her or his images are a trace of the route that she or he took. They tell us about the moments where her or his trajectory crossed over with the biographical journey of the objects photographed. They are, as such, a moment in the ongoing story of the repair and making of things. The objects' stories do not end when they are photographed or when they are repaired, but rather they continue beyond what it is that we can already know about them. They will be known by other hands, repaired with different tools, reformed, and re-made, as they move through the world and its temporalities.

The photographs in this book are sensorially rich. They evoke their objects in ways that invite us to draw on our own experiences of texture, light and environment, and to imagine what it would be like to hold and know them. These photographs invite us to participate for a moment in these stories, to view a moment from a present that is now in the past, and to use it to imagine histories and futures of making and repair.

References
1. T. Ingold, 'Introduction: The perception of the user-producer' in W. Gunn and J. Donovan (eds) *Design and Anthropology* (Farnham, Ashgate, 2012) 19–34.

Sarah Pink is Professor of Design and Media Ethnography at RMIT University, Australia, and Professor of Social Sciences at Loughborough University, UK. She is an interdisciplinary scholar whose academic and applied research draws on visual and sensory methodologies to understand how distinctive ways of knowing in the world are part of the ways people experience the present and imagine the future.

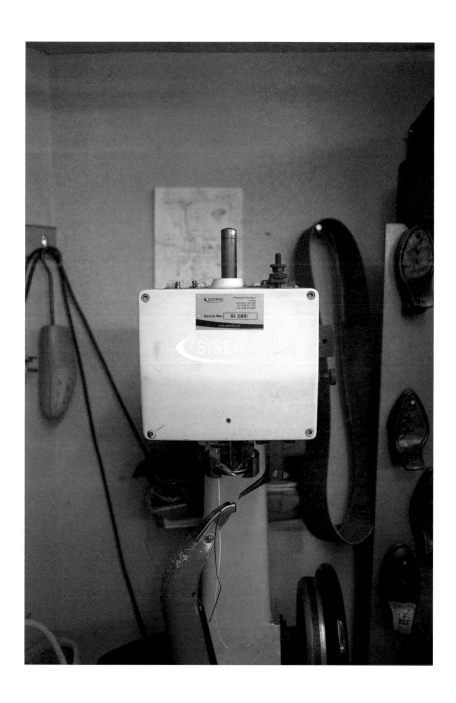

Photographs by Steven Bond

Bath Typewriter Service
Bath, Somerset
December 2011

Cane Corner
East Budleigh, Devon
January 2012

Honiton Clock Clinic
Honiton, Devon
April 2011

The Cycle Centre
Barnstaple, Devon
October 2011

*Michael Fook Small Engine
and Bicycle Repair*
South Molton, Devon
November 2011

Mount's Bay Electrical
Penzance, Cornwall
February 2012

*Helen Warren Porcelain
Repair*
Budleigh Salterton, Devon
February 2012

Sew-Quick
Falmouth, Cornwall
February 2011

Star Shoe Repairs
Redruth, Cornwall
April 2011

The Tool Box
Colyton, Devon
September 2011

Thompson Brothers
Bridgwater, Somerset
March 2009

New Life Upholstery
Barnstaple, Devon
October 2011

*F. W. Speller Boot & Shoe
Repairer*
Carharrack, Cornwall
February 2009

The Menders
Crewkerne, Somerset
November 2010

Castle Forge
Sherborne, Dorset
November 2010

R. Paveley, Tailor
Fortuneswell, Dorset
December 2010

*Jessica Rance Woodwind
Instrument Repairs*
Thornmoor Cross, Devon
February 2012

Biggleston's Hardware
Hayle, Cornwall
December 2010

The Abrams Bindery
Wellington, Somerset
January 2011

Stick of Lostwithiel
Lostwithiel, Cornwall
March 2012

Bath Typewriter Service

Bath Typewriter Service sits in a narrow building tacked on the end of a terrace of sandstone houses. Bill Collett has inhabited this workspace for more than three decades, servicing and mending typewriters as well as fax, adding and dictation machines of all shapes and sizes.

His main work station consists of three long desks, made by his father from three salvaged school blackboards. He used to work here with two colleagues, but their desks are no longer occupied. Bill works alone at the desk furthest from the door in a space resembling a homemade aircraft cockpit, where every implement, machine or tool is arranged within easy reach.

Machines once full of words and messages are now silent. The mechanical writing and recording machines of the past have been replaced with digital technologies, which are designed neither for servicing or repair. Much of Mr Collett's workshop is now taken up with old but perfectly operating machines which, rather than maintaining, he is breaking up into their constituent elements for scrap value: repair in reverse.

A lucky few, the most beautiful or rare, find a home with appreciative collectors. Many others sit on shelves, their fate undecided.

James R. Ryan

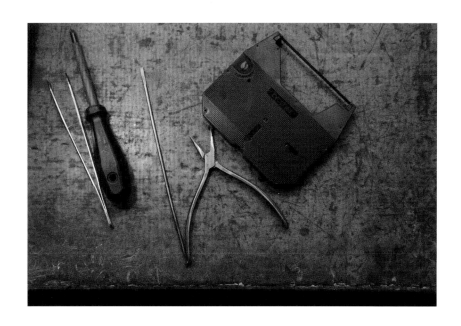

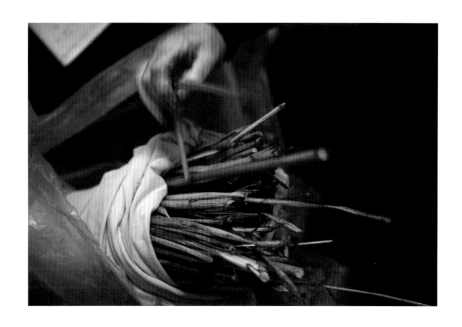

Cane Corner

The bundles of unworked rushes fill a stall-like space in the back room of Brigitte Graham's workshop, a former chicken coop repurposed to house her chair repair business. The bundles are rough, varied in hue, the stalks carrying a faint trace of their silty bed on the banks of the River Isle. In this state, the rushes seem earthy and unremarkable, unsure of how they could be useful. A makeshift toy spear? Padding for a swan's nest?

Then comes the transformation. Brigitte selects a rush from a bundle, testing it for the requisite pliability and strength. She draws the rush through her hands and twists it swiftly, then brings it towards the chair she is working on. The new rush is fastened to a loose rush from the worked seat, and twisted further as she works it into the pattern. She occasionally runs her hand down the as-yet untwisted trailing length to squeeze air pockets out of the spongy pith—they give way with a sharp pop. When the rush is bound tightly against others, what had been raw matter a moment ago is suddenly tamed, tucked into a neat formation. But the faint green of the new against the old signals the addition, the once-growing rush seeming somehow startled to find itself set into the seams of a human world.

Caitlin DeSilvey

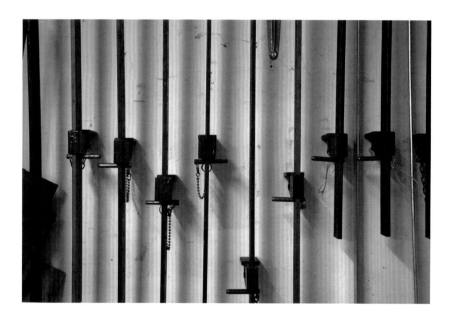

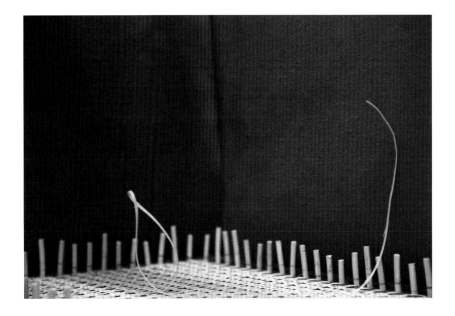

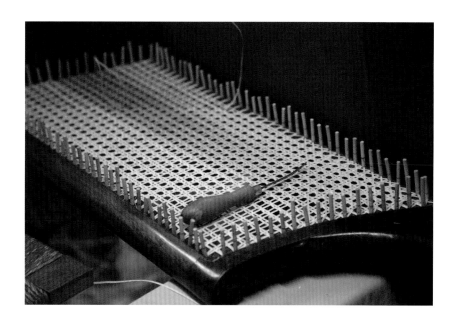

Honiton Clock Clinic

A dealer brought in this clock and asked that the mechanical workings be replaced with quartz. It's been hanging on the wall ever since. To restore the movement to the 150 year-old device would cost around £300; the quartz setting would be closer to £30. But it's not a question of whether the replacement can be done, it's whether the people who know how to do it are willing to, and they're not, not really. The clock—an ornate memento of the Crimean War—deserves better. There's an unwritten horologist's code of ethics at work here, which values the integrity of the piece more than the potential economic gain in its sale. So the clock hangs on the chipboard wall in one of the middle workshops, above a collection of necessary objects—cassette tape, 9-volt battery, specialist screwdrivers, a phone number.

The juxtaposition of the ordinary and the exquisite is repeated again and again in this space, and it's one of the qualities that makes the workshop so bewildering. Wild variations in scale add to the effect—the giant long-case clocks stacked three deep in cramped rooms, telescoping down to the screws and chains as thin as pins, their joints and threads only visible with a glass. The temporal scrambling is also unsettling—we were surrounded by dozens of clocks, but when I needed to know the time so that I could figure out whether I needed to go buy a new parking ticket I realised that none of them showed the same time. Cliff consulted a modern clock that seemed to be six hours off. It turns out the minute hand is accurate—radio-calibrated to the atomic clock in Rugby—but the hour hand went wrong some time back, and has never been re-set.

Caitlin DeSilvey

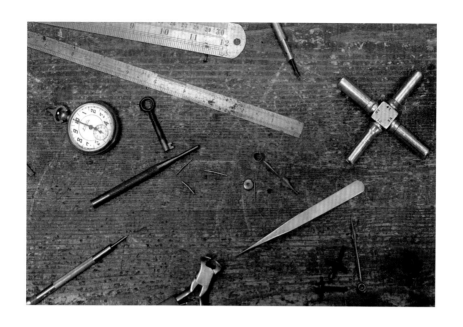

The Cycle Centre

Gordon Webber works outside, in all weathers and all seasons, on the pavement in front of a shop premises packed floor to ceiling with his collection of bicycles and bicycle parts. There is only just enough room for the door to swing in.

Gordy, as he is known by most, has been fixing bicycles in Barnstaple for almost 50 years. He got his start at the age of 11, when the receding waters from the Lynmouth floods left an array of parts and bicycles strewn along the riverbank near his home. He taught himself how to assemble a working bicycle from the stranded components, and took on an apprenticeship in a Barnstaple bike and buggy shop when he was 15.

After an eight-year apprenticeship he set himself up on his own. Now, the local 15 year-olds hang around his *en plein air* workshop on their own bikes, watching Gordy work. A collection of frequently-used tools leans against the curb, and a leaf drifts down to keep a ball bearing company.

Caitlin DeSilvey

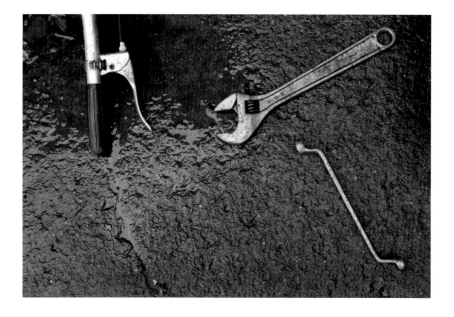

Michael Fook Small Engine and Bicycle Repair

Farley Water, Halscombe, Whiterocks, Veraby Brake, Venfield Common. An Exmoor geography dangles from each antler, marked on a neat white tag. The stags drop their antlers in March and April, and Michael Fook tries to be there to retrieve them. He can tell the stags apart, and recognise the distinctive patterning of each individual's antler structure from year to year. If only one antler is dropped he will wait, and search for the missing mate. Sometime he finds it miles away, and once he swapped with a local acquaintance years later to make two matched sets.

The antlers return, in pairs and singly, to Michael's shop in South Molton, Devon. In the front of the shop a dozen prime specimens are mounted (on fibreglass skulls) around the walls, sharing space with spare bicycle tyres and rims. More cluster around the edges of the floor space, the handlebars of parked bicycles echoing the antler forms to odd effect. In the high-ceilinged workshop at the back antlers hang above the strimmers and mowers in for repair.

Caitlin DeSilvey

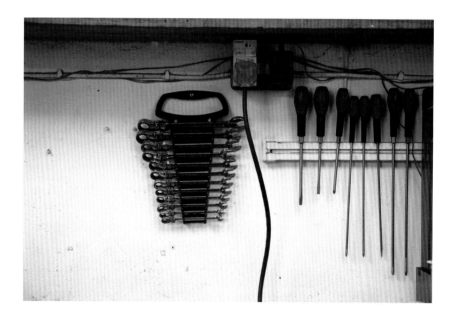

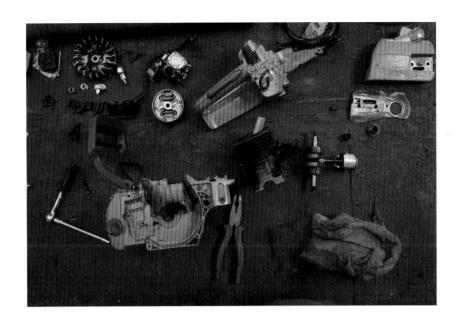

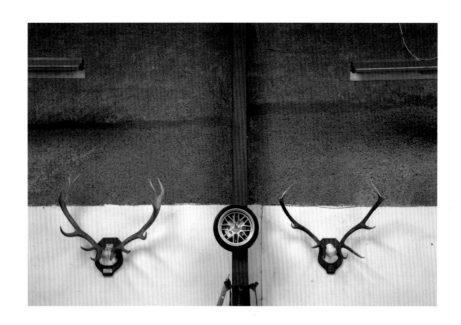

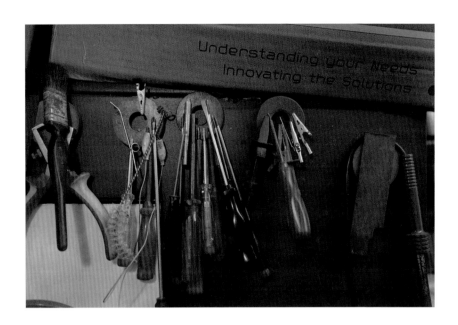

Mount's Bay Electrical

The problems presented at Mount's Bay Electrical on one rainy Penzance morning are various. A vacuum cleaner isn't sucking properly. A small motor needs looking at. An electric shaver is making a strange noise. A woman brings in a friend's kettle that "keeps blowing the trip off". Jeff unfastens the base to look at the kettle element and breaks the news that repair, in this case, is not going to be worthwhile.

The measure of *worthwhile*: a calculation made swiftly, dozens of times a day, a different answer every time. Relevant variables include the quality of the appliance, the expense of parts (if they are even available), the time required to carry out the repair and fuzzier metrics of customer habit and attachment. One Hoover in for servicing—slack-bagged and beige—has been returning periodically to Jeff for close to 25 years. Another unremarkable vacuum cleaner specimen is collected by its owner for the cost of a £20 repair: "Wonderful", she says.

Caitlin DeSilvey

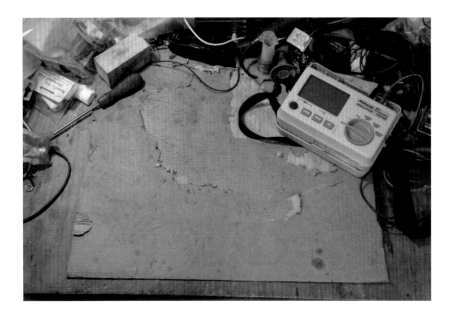

Helen Warren Porcelain Repair

The photograph captures her reaching upward, looking inward, only air where her right hand should be. A faint smile plays on her lips. She wears her wounds lightly, a cap and shawl of masking tape somehow only accentuating her causal elegance and the flawless plane of her bared midriff. What happened? A knock from a high shelf? A carelessly packed shipping carton? She has come to Helen Warren's workshop to be repaired, to be made whole again. But there are decisions—aesthetic, ethical, and practical—to be made about how the repair will be done, and what our lady will look like when she goes home. Helen's own words best express the distinction between 'conservation' and 'restoration', display and disguise:

"Conservation techniques aim to preserve and stabilise items for later use without seeking to disguise evidence of the original damage. A typical 'museum' type of repair would include cleaning and re-assembling broken shards to reconstruct the original shape. Some re-touching may also be necessary but the break lines would still be visible. Restoration aims to disguise damaged areas and bring an object back to its original state by re-building or modelling missing areas, repairing and repainting. This must be carried out sympathetically with materials compatible with the object. Ethical considerations and use of reversible products are a priority in all cases of restoration."

Caitlin DeSilvey

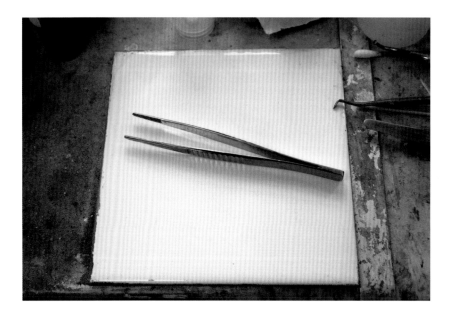

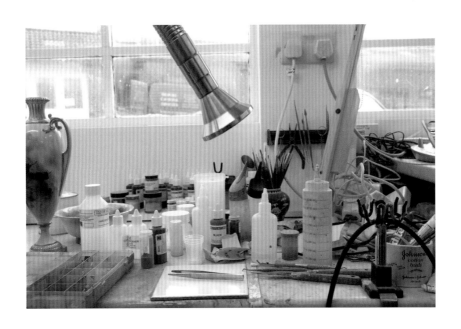

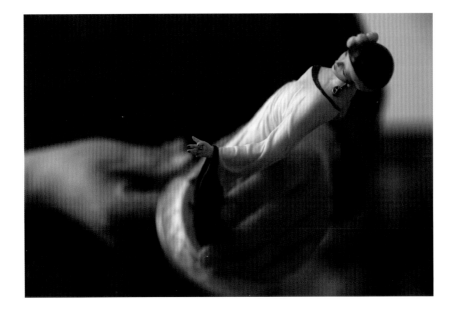

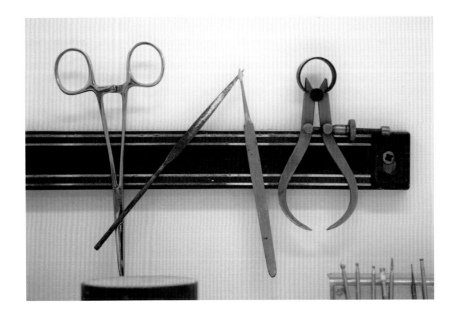

Sew-Quick

Sew-Quick is a thriving industrial and domestic sewing machine service located on a mostly residential back street in an old light-industrial building. The workshop itself is divided roughly into two separate spaces separated by a thin wall, with a large opening to one side. The space at the back of the workshop contains a workbench, shelves of machinery, tools and equipment. It is here that sewing machines are made and mended.

The area at the front of the shop is where Sue or Francis (and their dog) greet customers; it is the 'shop' bit of the 'workshop'. A small enclosure to the back right of this space serves as a rudimentary office, with a counter behind which Sue or Francis can use the phone, receive payments and issue receipts or sell small sewing machine parts. It is here that the day-to-day collection or deposition of sewing machines goes on.

The space to the right and front of the counter is completely occupied by a number of large industrial sewing machines. To the left of the counter, running along the length of the wall and in front of one of the building's large and drafty windows, are some large wooden shelves on which are stored more sewing machines, as well as all kinds of other useful clutter. These spaces speak a language of everyday work in which people and objects are entangled in complex ways. Arrangements of objects and spaces are organised less on the basis of visual display than on the need of getting things done.

James R. Ryan

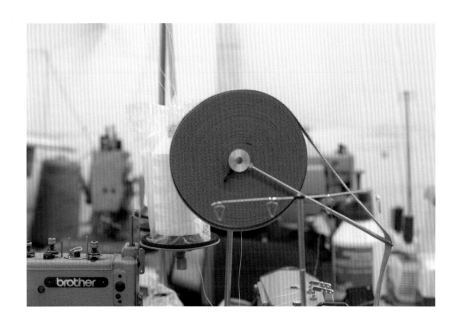

Star Shoe Repairs

There is so much to look at in this place that it is hard to remember all the details; the photographs show things noticed and forgotten, but also things not seen at all at the time. A large pair of scissors secured to back of the side of the worktop by an improvised leather holster; the wire brush drill-bit resting on a shelf; racks of keys and metal cutting blades pinned to a wooden panels; a stripy window display of handmade leather belts; a women's shoe secured in a home-made heel-clamp.

The wooden display rack for 'Wren's Super-Wax Shoe Polish', with its gold-lettered strap-line: "Keeps Shoes Supple", radiates an aura of quality and craftsmanship. It sits against the pink paintwork, alongside a lonely single shoe, a roll of cotton, and assorted leather bits and bobs, on a high shelf in the corner of the workshop.

The photograph conjures up a miniaturised landscape, the wooden sign resembling some mid-twentieth-century wayside advert set in jumbled ground and bathed in the evening glow of a permanently setting fluorescent-light-bulb-sun. Such aesthetic games are of course an effect of the frame imposed by the camera. But the invitation to play with a sense of scale and perspective comes also from the multi-sensory and visually rich quality of such workplaces, with their abundance of juxtapositions and quirky associations of shapes, textures, colours and objects.

James R. Ryan

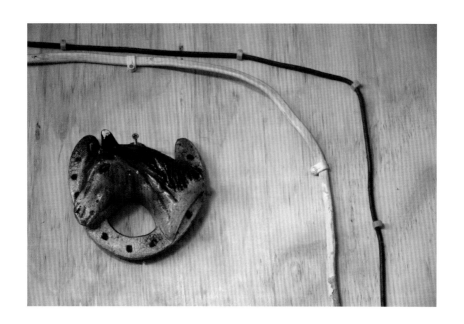

The Tool Box

Engineers use scribing blocks like this one to etch lines at set heights and to judge the level of the surfaces they are working on. A row of these blocks sits on a high shelf in David Fouracre's used tool shop. They fall into a category of 'tools that are used to make other tools', though someone needs to make them in the first place. David speculated that Mike Hill (the name etched on side of the block) made this particular scribing block as an 'apprentice piece' during his training.

Many of the tools in this shop have makers marks which identify the people who made them and the places where they were made. An idiosyncratic industrial geography can be read in the rows of clamps and planes, chisels and drill bits. The tools also carry marks of their working lives, nicks and dings and scratches accumulated over years of use and wear. They arrive battered and grubby, and undergo a transformation at the hands of Michael in the back room workshop. Restored and ready on the shop's display shelves, they await their next posting.

Caitlin DeSilvey

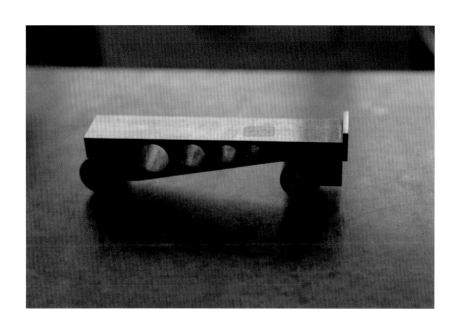

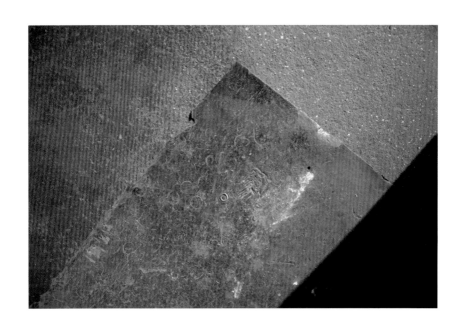

Thompson Brothers

A wave of brown lino washes over the Robin's Red concrete floor, the lino's surface imprinted with an accidental archive. We sense the ironmonger standing behind the long counter, waiting for the presentation of a need—the roofing felt that wants tacking on, the missing bolt, the loose strut. As he works through the years, a small rain of stray tacks, pins, staples and screws falls from the counter to the floor below. The ironmonger shifts, and the sole of his shoe presses the object into the lino. Occasionally, he bends to retrieve the lost things, or to sweep them back into circulation. The traces are like tiny fossils, shadows of motion and material.

The photograph records one of the places that seeded this project: Thompson Brothers Ironmongers. Thompson Brothers traded continuously for 210 years, until Peter Bond finally closed up shop in August 2009. He felt the increase of internet shopping, combined with the burgeoning effects of a 'throw-away society', rendered the business unsustainable. "There is no longer enough demand for quality tools and materials that last", he laments. The photographs record the store's last days, as the family packed up and prepared the remaining stock for auction.

Caitlin DeSilvey

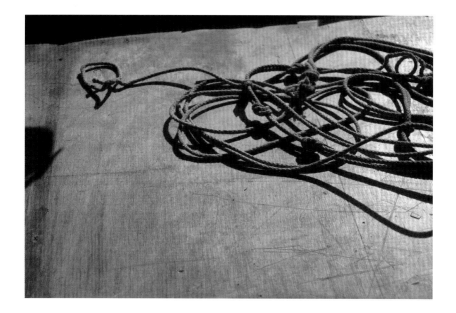

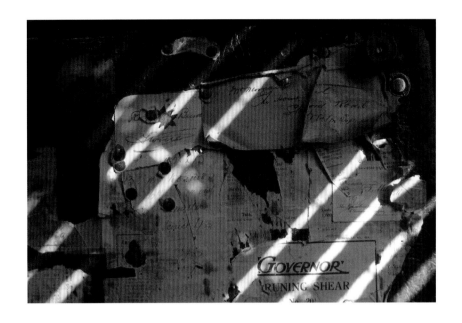

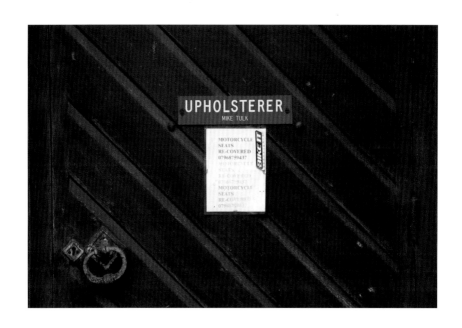

New Life Upholstery

Mike was waiting for us in his tiny workshop, which is wedged in under the wing of a former church, now antique shop. The sign out front said 'Upholsterer, Mike Tulk', in white on red. Another teapot-shaped sign said 'Tea Room: Sorry no tea, but upholstery gladly done'. Mike was having a slow week, his 'bread and butter' business of recovering motorbike seats having temporarily dried up.

He showed us the tools of his trade: a pair of pincers to loosen the seat cover staples, a screwdriver to pry them out, and two venerable sewing machines. One of them is a crank-operated Jones model from the 1930s. Mike has fixed a £1.99 torch onto the working end so that he can see the piping foot clearly as he stitches up seams, but the light flickers and fades. He thinks it may be the damp in the stone-floored room.

Caitlin DeSilvey

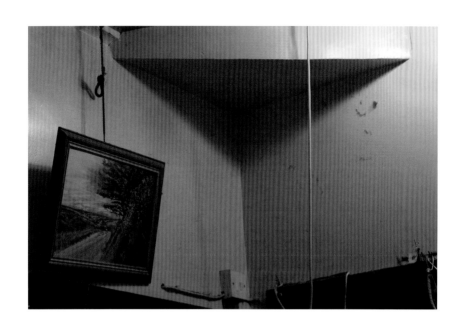

F. W. Speller Boot & Shoe Repairer

William Speller established his boot and shoe repair business in 1930, and trained his two sons, Stephen and Frederick, to join him. The three of them worked together until Stephen eventually became the sole proprietor in the 1970s. People in the village kept bringing him their repairs through the 1980s, and Stephen oiled the machines faithfully once a week long after his jobs wound down.

He died in February 2008, at the age of 92. Stephen's niece, Myrna Croome, who inherited the cottage, began to contact local museums, hoping to find someone to take on the contents of the workshop for display. By the time we were put in touch with her in December she had almost given up; her builder was eager to demolish the shed to begin work on the new water system, and time was running out. Myrna met us at the cottage and we walked through the half-gutted rooms to the narrow back yard.

The four of us crowded into the two-room clapboard shed, the tiny rooms separated by a half-door. The immediate impression was one of extreme density—a space fully occupied by the accretions of several decades of labour. Shelves and drawers lined the walls, tools hung in ordered rows, shoes nestled against each other next to the raw materials of their repair and the machinery gleamed in the dim light. I noted details—shoe sole packets scribbled with notes, the dated advertisements on the walls, the 1975 job price list tacked inside the door.

The place seemed to be waiting for someone to return, to pick up the letters and bills scattered on the workbench, to sit on the swivel chair and finish tacking on a stray heel.

Caitlin DeSilvey

The Menders

The workspace at the back of the shop, on first glance, seems chaotic, but the order becomes apparent with explanation. Shoes in to be mended start their journey in the 'day boxes', indicating the day of the week on which they will begin their transformation from worn to reborn.

The 'benching' process comes first, which involves carrying out any necessary stitching, resoling or replacement of material. Once the major work is done the shoe goes in the 'benched up' box, before moving on for buffing and brightening on the finisher, which dominates one whole wall of the cramped space. As a final flourish, Ali inks a distinctive pattern on the sole of each shoe. "Ali's an artist", says Simon, the owner of the shop. As he talks to us about his work, Ali leans against the finisher, his body held against the functional curve of the bulky device, in his element.

Caitlin DeSilvey

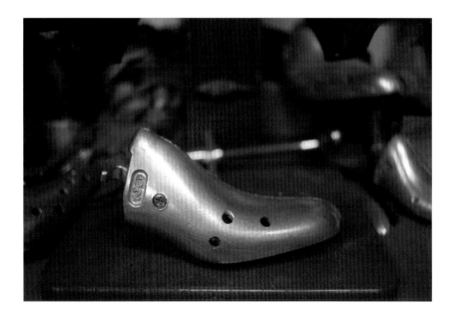

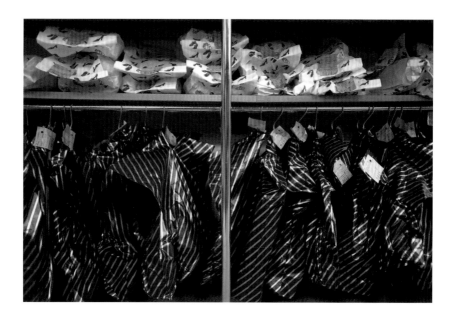

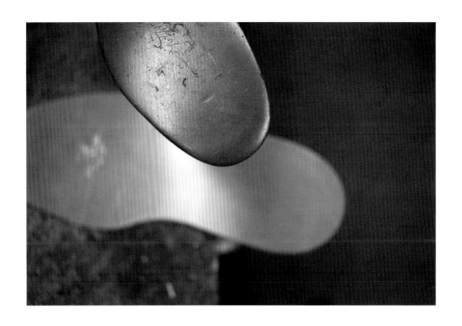

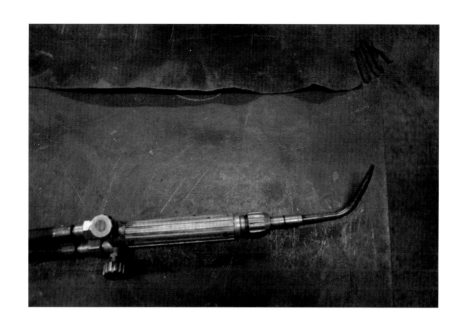

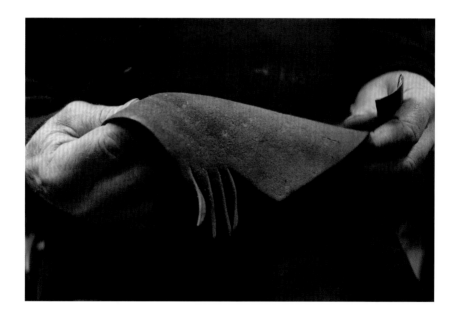

Castle Forge

When we visited Steve Willdig at his forge in Sherborne, below the castle walls, he told us a story about King Solomon. It went something like this:

King Solomon brought together all of the guilds to determine who was the best craftsman in the land. The tailor was chosen, and the blacksmith left town in protest. In the blacksmith's absence the community began to unravel—the tailor couldn't sharpen his shears, the farmer's tools weren't mended. St Dunstan was sent out to find the blacksmith, and at a banquet the smith was named 'craftsman of all craftsmen'. During the meal the spiteful tailor snuck under the table and cut a fringe on the edge of the blacksmith's apron.

The story offers an allegory of Steve's own understanding of his work, his worth and his place in his community. "I've been looking after Sherborne for 30 years", he remarked. Steve tells many stories of his own, but he also listens to the stories that people bring him along with the objects that need his attention—the older couple with the favourite porridge pot that needs a new handle, the woman who needs a rack on the back of the chair "just there" so she can hang her dish towel. Sometimes, Steve gently suggests that the story is more important than the repair—the copper jug dented by a reckless grandchild—and the dent remains. "You have to be careful not to erase the stories."

Caitlin DeSilvey

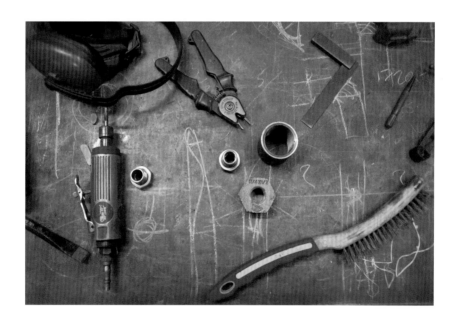

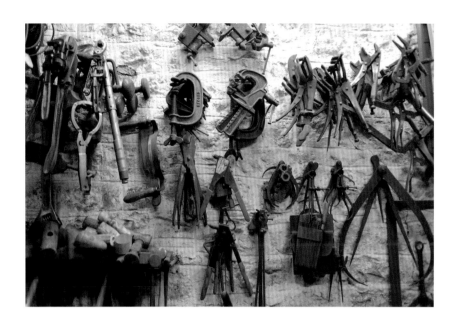

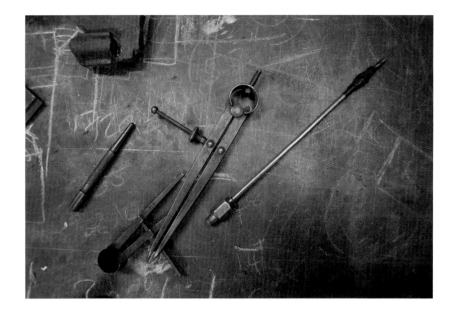

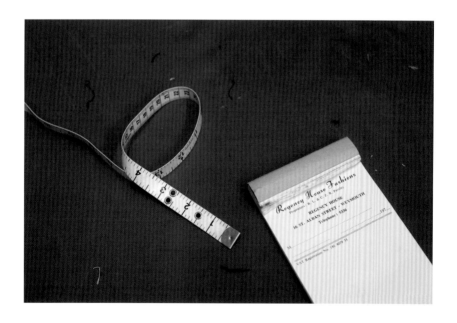

R. Paveley, Tailor

The receipt book lay at the edge of the cutting table, in a drift of short threads and fabric scraps. Regency House Fashions, Weymouth, closed down in around 1990, when Reg Paveley's tailoring empire (which once stretched to Birmingham as well) contracted to the storefront at the crook of Fore Street, Fortuneswell, Portland. The sign out front says "established 1946", the year Mr Paveley set himself up in the trade, at age 20, though far from this bulky isle.

Other things on the cutting table—three pairs of jeans in for taking up and hemming; 'donkeys' (fabric-covered boards, used for pressing); two huge pairs of steel shears (one made in Newark, New Jersey; and the other made in Sheffield).

When I look at these images they pull me back into the tone and the texture of the place, and talk back to the old documentary impulse, reminding me that we only ever have pieces of the imaginary whole —short threads—to work with.

Caitlin DeSilvey

Jessica Rance Woodwind Instrument Repairs

A ring of rare black wood, harvested from the African Grenadilla tree. A bit of old wine bottle cork. A cutting from a sheet of industrial nickel-silver. An eyeless needle. An ivory billiard ball, and the green baize cloth from the table it may have once travelled. In Jessica Rance's workshop these things are reborn. Tenons for a broken clarinet. Trill key bumpers. New keys, and the springs to hold their tension. Ivory mounts for a bassoon or an oboe. Felt pads to protect the wood from the pressure of the keys.

The transformations are accomplished with the help of an extended family of tools and machines—Leonard the lathe, Mildred the milling machine, Einstein the jig tool, the screwdriver with the blackwood handle that Jess made (forging the steel herself) in college, a battered and beloved mallet. Repair is collaborative, a joint project of matter and machine, musician and mender. The instruments have names as well. Basil the bassoon, Clarence the clarinet, Arthur the upright piano. They share the workshop with Leonard and Mildred, and also share some their functional identity. "At the end of the day these beautiful things are machines, and if they are well-made machines, they will last."

Caitlin DeSilvey

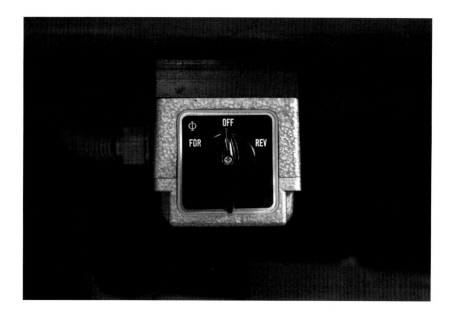

Biggleston's Hardware

One of the first things you notice about the interior of Biggleston's, besides the faint aroma of mothballs and paraffin that infuses all proper and longstanding hardware stores, is the vast array of boxes. Wooden and cardboard boxes of various sizes, containing all kinds of hardware necessities, climb up the shelves that cover the far wall and line all sides of a small room beyond.

The most striking of these are the substantial wooden boxes, covered by a flakey, goose-shit-green paint, that sit at head height. The fronts of the boxes carry specimens of hardware as well as hand-written, brown paper labels which hint at each box's contents: 'Glass plates'; 'Rack pulleys'; 'Fancy Hinges'. The boxes were salvaged in the 1920s after the closure of the National Explosive Works at 'Dynamite Towans' on the edge of Hayle, which had employed over 1500 local workers at its height in WW1.

The peeling paper labels were written and affixed by Mr Hodge, a previous proprietor of Biggleston's. They don't always predict accurately the boxes' contents and some ('D6', 'E3', 'F4') are written entirely in a lost language of stock and storage. Even Ray Wyse, the present proprietor, is uncertain of their meaning. But, these boxes, like the shop they fill, are valued not just for their utility but also for their significance as historical artifacts and carriers of collective memory.

James R. Ryan

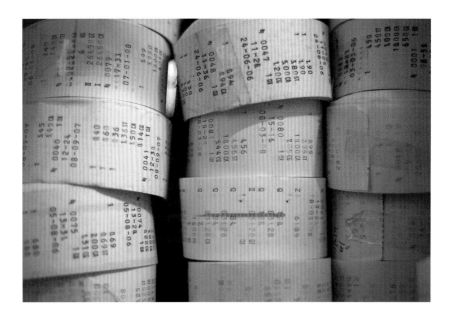

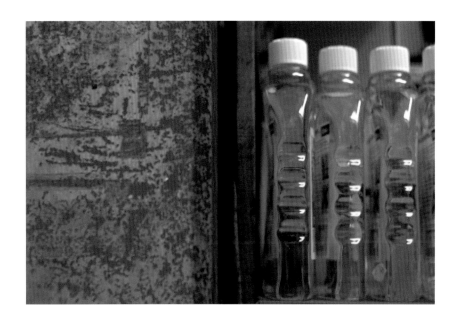

The Abrams Bindery

If a photograph is always 'about' something, then this one seems to be about gravity, and light. The iron weight compresses a book's newly-fastened boards, the winter sun glances in before heading west. Maybe it is also about time—the time it takes to do a job well, to take a broken thing and make it whole. Weight. Wait. When we visited in January, Alexander Abrams and his son Nicholas were working on jobs that had been brought into their bindery in May of the previous year. They were rebinding, among other things, Leach's 1815 monograph on *British Crabs, Lobsters, Prawns and other Crustacea*, and an illustrated text on *Figures of Mosaic Pavements discovered at Horkston in Lincolnshire*, published in 1801.

I brought them some books of my own which had endured generations of tough love: pages were torn and scribbled-on, boards pulled away from the stitching. Alexander took one look at my little pile and informed me, kindly, that their repair wouldn't be 'economic'. I thought about how it would feel to get rid of these books, and decided that I was willing to invest in having them saved. I left the books at the bindery, and when I return to collect them they will have been transformed, their use-value eclipsed by their exchange-value. I'll buy new copies for my son, and these will live on a precious-things shelf. There is loss in this transformation, and also gain, as the biography of the books becomes bound up with other forms of value—not least value of the skills needed to fix them.

Caitlin DeSilvey

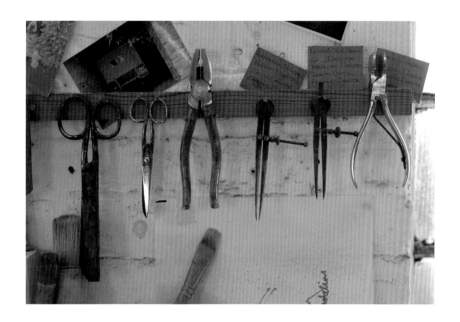

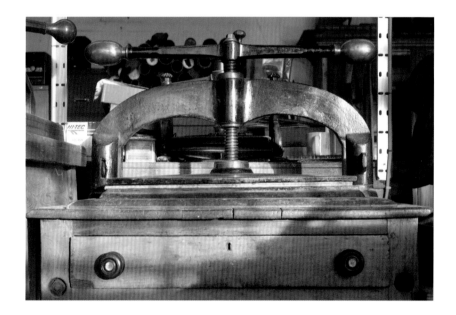

Stick of Lostwithiel

Stick of Lostwithiel was the first business that we visited as part of the project, and also the last. The floods that arrived suddenly in Lostwithiel in November 2010, shortly after our first visit, ruined many businesses in the town. Stick, a specialist shop repairing all kinds of leather goods and selling shoes, belts, hats and walking sticks, was particularly badly hit by the floodwater, depriving Graham and Rosemary Mitson of their shop and home for over a year.

On our return in March 2012 the space feels welcoming and settled, certainly not like somewhere so recently, and so dramatically, deluged. The workbench where Graham Mitson examines and fixes the numerous objects that customers bring to his shop now sits squarely in the main shop space. Its design and arrangement of neatly organised implements and materials reflects the craftsman's affection for the hand-made and utilitarian. The brightly-coloured metal and enamel Dunlop Boots advertisement, like the museum cabinet with antique shoes on the back wall of the shop, reminds the visitor that this is not simply a place to buy new things, but an opportunity to learn from accumulated knowledge of crafting and repair.

The material memories present in the shop almost two years ago seem not only present but also amplified. Like a pair of favourite shoes, Stick has been lovingly repaired, its place in the local universe restored.

James R. Ryan

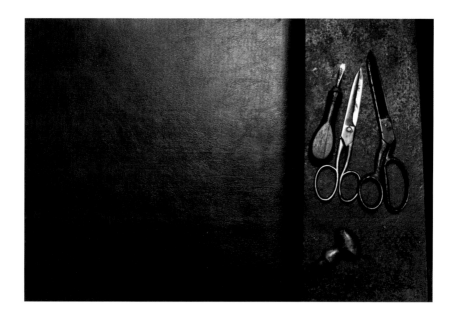

Caitlin DeSilvey & James R. Ryan

Geography, photography and repair: we calmly and adventurously go travelling

By close-ups of the things around us, by focusing on hidden details of familiar objects, by exploring commonplace milieus under the ingenious guidance of the camera, the film, on the one hand, extends our comprehension of the necessities which rule our lives; on the other hand, it manages to assure us of an immense and unexpected field of action. Our taverns and our metropolitan streets, our offices and furnished rooms, our railroad stations and our factories appeared to have us locked up hopelessly. Then came the film and burst this prison-world asunder by the dynamite of the tenth of a second, so that now, in the midst of its far-flung ruins and debris, we calmly and adventurously go travelling. With the close-up, space expands; with slow motion, movement is extended. The enlargement of a snapshot does not simply render more precise what in any case was visible, though unclear: it reveals entirely new structural formations of the subject.[1]
—Walter Benjamin

In September 2010 we embarked on an adventure. We had secured funding for a project to investigate the visual and material cultures associated with the making and mending of everyday objects in the South West. We called our endeavour 'Small is Beautiful?' (with a nod to E. F. Schumacher), though we soon shortened it to 'SiB'. For two years, we travelled—adventurously, but not always calmly. We moved around the region on trains and in rental cars, seeking out places where people were fixing things. Our travels took us to market town high streets and front parlour studios, cold garages and sleepy suburban streets, industrial estates and converted stables. Along the way we met some amazing people, who were grounded in their communities and their vocations.

Steven, for the most part, didn't take photographs of the people we met—except sometimes their hands. Instead, he photographed the spaces where they worked and the materials they worked with, the "hidden details of familiar objects" and the "commonplace milieus". His framing was often extremely close up, focusing on materials, textures and objects. On each of our workplace visits, Steven was accompanied by one of us, so our documentation was textual as well as visual—conversations scribbled in a notebook, stories about things and people. The words were later assembled into short essays and texts, published on our blog, set in relation with selected images.

We like to think that our travels shared something of the spirit of the collaboration that developed in the summer of 1936 between writer James Agee and photographer Walker Evans, who turned their sojourn with Alabama sharecroppers into the strange and wonderful book, *Let Us Now Praise Famous Men*. In the introduction Agee wrote, "The photographs are not illustrative. They, and the text, are coequal, mutually independent, and fully collaborative".[2] The words that opened this essay were written by Walter Benjamin, also in 1936. It seems somehow significant that these three men—Benjamin in Paris, and Agee and Evans in Alabama—were, in the same historical moment, trying to make sense of a world gripped by prolonged financial crisis by turning back to older forms of practice and perception (while simultaneously critiquing their attraction to these forms, and not quite trusting it). The moment resonates. In 2010, we found ourselves carrying out our research against a background of economic recession, which seemed to have sparked a renaissance of 'make do and mend' activity among younger people, and more demand for repair services generally.

The Small is Beautiful? project also came out of a particular moment in the wider field of cultural geography. In the past couple of decades, geographers have spent a fair amount of time talking about the relationship between geography and visual culture, and geography and art. Geographers have made a significant contribution to critical and textual readings of visual material, attentive to politics and iconography. More recently, we've seen a focus on collaborative practice, with geographers working alongside artists, or integrating creative visual methodologies into their own work. This project sits somewhere in this development, but with its explicit focus on visual *and* material cultures, it also extends into a relatively new area of enquiry for geography. This kind of thinking and working has been going on in other disciplines for some time now, particularly anthropology, exemplified by the work of Sarah Pink on visual and sensory methodologies.[3]

Last year Gillian Rose and Divya Tolia-Kelly, two geographers who have thought a good deal about images and things, published an edited volume titled *Visuality/Materiality*. They introduced the volume with a "manifesto for practice", which insisted that the visual is always also embodied and material, and that the material is always tangled with the optical and the imaged. Research, they argued, needs to try to understand the cultural practices that "make things visible in specific ways", and move away from a focus on signification and meaning, towards a messier, more implicated and situated, interpretive stance.[4]

Rose and Tolia-Kelly's focus was on "visual and material research that unravels, disturbs and connects with *processes, embodied practices* and *technologies…*".[5] They did not provide much detail about how to go about actually doing this kind of research, however. So, in the rest of this essay, we consider how our research set about making things visible in specific ways, as well as how we made the making itself (their making, and our making) visible, and tangible. We do this by using the rubric proposed by Rose and Tolia-Kelly—working through processes, technologies and practices.

Processes

Reflecting on the project, the process that seemed to dominate much of our time was *sorting*. We sorted through categories of objects, and types of places, and slowly developed a set of criteria that helped us decide whether or not to include a particular site in the project. We also, eventually, sorted the images themselves, in attending to their display and dissemination.

In the beginning, our criteria were loose. We knew we were interested in 'everyday' objects rather than exceptional items, but the category of the everyday is sufficiently slippery that it usually raised more questions than it answered. We also knew we wanted to focus on practices of repair and mending, rather than the crafting of original pieces. Eventually, we hit on the consumption conundrum. If you can hold a broken thing in your hand and ask yourself, "Should I buy a new one for £7 (or £70), or find someone who can fix this?", then the object made the cut. We soon became adept at using our repair-based taxonomy to sort objects as suitable or not: clocks but not cars; toasters but not tractors. We became sharply aware early on that the project was working against a powerful tide of induced obsolescence—most objects are no longer made to be repaired. Even so, by the end of the project, the repaired objects we had encountered

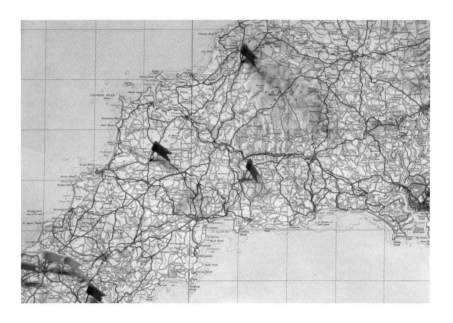

included: shoes; clothes; books; sewing machines; motorcycle seats; ironwork; clocks and watches; typewriters; small electrical appliances; musical instruments; bicycles; small engines; ceramics; and cane chairs. Ordinary objects shared space with extraordinary ones: rare books; dress shoes crafted from trout-skin; a mirrored crystal Crimean War commemorative clock. Someone's everyday, perhaps, but not ours. The project made us aware of the irony that repair in the present day is often a lifestyle choice (and a luxury) rather than a necessity—as it is for most of the world.

Once we decided what objects we were interested in we needed to sort out the different establishments we would work with. Our progress was charted on an office wall map (*detail, above*), yellow flag for yes, red flag for no, blue for maybe and yellow for completed. This was a collaborative process as well. Selecting the sites was not just about our discernment, but was also dependent on the receptivity of the people who worked in these places. Some people immediately recognised what we were doing (or thought they did, even if we weren't sure ourselves) and others didn't. Interestingly, the word 'repair' wasn't always that helpful. The people who thought of themselves primarily as 'makers' acted as if they had been waiting for us to show up, for someone to recognise the value of their work. They made it clear that they thought of what they did as much more than simple repair. For them it was about problem-solving, invention, innovation, social work, service. The people who didn't have time for us—although we didn't speak to them at length—didn't seem to have the same sense of their work as creative labour, as a valuable and valid object of a research project. Several of the shops we worked with had been approached by photographers before, indicating that the aesthetic that we were after was, to a certain extent, a shared one.

There were other processes of sorting at work within the project, carried out by the shopkeepers themselves. Several times every day a customer would come to them with a broken object, and preface their appeal with, "I don't suppose you could do anything about…". At this point the person behind the counter had to make a calculation about whether the repair was, literally, worth their while. This calculation was made swiftly, but confidently. Relevant variables include the quality of the appliance, the expense of the necessary parts (if they were even available) and the time required to carry out the repair. Once a quote was given—or the customer was gently informed that repair was "not economic"—softer variables of emotional or practical attachment came into play. Often, the customer decided to pay for the repair anyway, extending the life of a family clock handed down through the generations, or a favourite pair of jeans.

Finally, the project involved the sorting of the images. The images were saved as files on Steven's camera, then transferred to his computer where he carried out an initial rough sort (a process sometimes shared by us, but mostly not). We selected a single image from each site to include on our project blog (more on this below), but we also began the process of sorting the images prior to their display. Particular images caught our eyes, and the more we looked the more common themes and narratives suggested themselves in relation to certain photographs. The photographs seemed to want to be together, in pairs or triplets, and then in series. These relationships were remarkably durable and resonant, and oddly familial: our shorthand for these arrangements was 'SiBlings'.

There is some alignment here with the Bechers' "families of objects", their categorisation of industrial infrastructure. There are also affinities with Geoff Dyer's idiosyncratic and incidental account of photography, *The Ongoing Moment*, where he immerses himself, like piece of sensitised material, within collections of photographs and responds to the patterns and stories that emerge. Like Dyer, who borrows from Henri Cartier-Bresson, we sought to use photographs as "a way of comprehending".[6] Our families of images travelled—to four exhibitions and two conferences over 16 months, from Kendal, Cumbria to St Austell, Cornwall. The exhibition gradually grew as the project went on, and each show became the occasion for a public

conversation about the project and its wider context. Finally, Steven sorted through the images again to create montages for display on the project website, and for inclusion in this book.

Technologies

Having described some of the sorting that was involved in the project we now move on to the next mode of engagement: technologies. To return to Agee, again, "The immediate instruments are two: the motionless camera and the printed word".[7] Steven's camera mediated our experience of each site, and was the pretext for our presence there. We acted mostly as Steven's accomplices, distracting the people in the shop so he could roam where his eye took him.

Often, however, the people in the shops had their own lines of enquiry to pursue. Several of the people we met were amateur photographers themselves—Mike Fook showed us his thick photo albums of the stags he stalked on Exmoor, and Bill Collett kept a portrait studio in an upstairs room. They wanted to talk cameras with Steven, to compare equipment and technique. The camera was set in this context as one instrument of many—the broken things brought in for repair, the tools used to return them to working order. The musical instrument repairer we worked with commented: "At the end of the day these beautiful things are machines, and if they are well-made machines they will last".[8]

Once we started thinking seriously about display, other decisions about appropriate technology came into play. We decided early on to explore what it would mean to treat the exhibited photographs as objects in their own right, with a material as well as a visual presence in the world. For our first series, seven sets of three, we mounted the prints on 3mm aluminium. This involved complex deliberations with a printer in Exeter, and the prints were sent to Yeovil for mounting, where some random but necessary cropping occurred. We then created a set of 21 tiny shelves, using aluminium architrave with a conventional application in shower installations. A later set of five images was printed on large sheets of canvas. Sorting out the technicalities of hanging these 'flags' involved three return visits to an Exeter ironmongery. At the exhibitions, we encouraged people to touch and handle the photographs that were mounted on aluminium, to know them with their hands as well as their eyes. These, as well as the larger prints and the flags, accumulated signs of their movement through the world—scratches and dents, nicks and smudges.

We went to these lengths to stress a commitment to the photograph as something *made*, and to draw out the parallels between our making and the making we encountered in the places we documented. Like the people with whom we worked, we made choices about materials and processes, and applied (and acquired) skills through the process of completing certain tasks. Steven's expertise in the photographic craft was essential to this process, and we wanted

to make this visible in the work. After we presented the research at a conference someone in the audience asked why we didn't take our own photographs, or ask the people in the shops to take the photographs? We didn't, we responded, for the same reason we don't fix our own shoes. The photographs were not merely secondary records, illustrations for our text, but always intended as new expressions and commentaries in their own right.

We also tried to be continually aware of the way the tools and instruments we were using affected what we were looking at. Our attention produced these places, and made them visible, in particular ways. The lingering spectre of hazy sentimentality and nostalgia was an aspect of this project with which we engaged cautiously from the start. Connecting to our wider interests, the photographs became a space for reflecting on and acknowledging an inherited aesthetic around outmoded objects and picturesque decline. The photographs, made and managed with highly specialised digital technology, introduced a tension, a critical remove, that allowed us to make sense of our own attraction to these places, and to situate it both politically and poetically. We found that even apparently 'nostalgic' engagements can provide opportunities to assert alternative sets of values in opposition to dominant economic and social orders— moving beyond just market and use value to acknowledge emotional, ethical and aesthetic value as well. The project, for us, was as much about transition as it was about tradition.

Finally, there were technologies of writing at work here as well. Initially, each site was the subject of a 'field frame' on the project blog: a short essay, written in response to a single image. The immediacy of the on-line forum, and constraints around length and audience, influenced our voice, and our observations. Edited versions of these pieces are included in this book, to introduce each site. We also carried out other experiments with text and image. For the display of the original '21' we produced micro-essays for each photo, confined to a text box of about 100 words, printed on a separate sheet, to be read alongside the images.[9]

These experiments gave us a powerful sense of words as objects with a specific size and volume, taking up space in particular ways. In the writing we did for the project, we learned not to expect the images to align with our notes and the observations we had made in these spaces. Steven didn't tend to photograph the things we'd noticed, necessarily, and the things he did photograph often looked unfamiliar, difficult to place. As American photographer Dorothea Lange famously noted, "the camera is an instrument that teaches people how to see without a camera".[10] Accordingly, we found that we needed to occupy the space of the image and let the observations arise from that dialogue. The images pulled us back into the tone and the texture of these places, revealing other forms of knowledge. As Benjamin phrased it, "The enlargement of a snapshot does not simply render more precise what in any case was visible, though unclear: it reveals entirely new structural formations of the subject".[11]

Embodied practices

We turn now to our third and final interpretative cut through the project, namely around the embodied practices we observed, and in which we participated. In some sense, these embodied engagements are the most difficult aspects of our research to describe. In each of the workshops, a precise and idiosyncratic arrangement of bodies and things was dictated by the requirements of the work carried out there and the preferences and particularities of the people who did the work. These spaces were dense with what Tim Dant describes as "material interaction", complex mappings of intention—the intention of the workers, and that embedded in their tools. In the blacksmith's shop, the triangulated space of forge/bench/anvil hummed with potential. In the clock-repair shop, individual work benches presented a magnified field of action for the minute repairs carried out there. Many of the photos capture the 'perceptual field' of the worker's body—the bench with the project spread out, the tools ready to hand.[12] The tools themselves are invariably shaped to invite handling and bodily mobilisation. The bodies of the workers in the images are absent presences, the arrangement of materials signalling their competence and their skilled relationship with the things they manipulate and maintain. The bookbinder commented of the slim white tool he uses to fold paper (*opposite*), "When I die I'll be holding my bone folder".[13]

We of course inserted our own presence into this physical world of the workshop, subtly altering the usual chemistry that existed between the workers and their tools. Our own intervention, armed with pen and notebook, was modest compared to the corporeal intervention required on the part of the photographer. Driven by his framing eye and imagination, Steven would throw himself into all manner of positions behind his camera, climbing ladders or crouching on the floor. His pictures of each place were in this way generated from a complex choreography of camera and photographer across the spaces of the workshop.

Other embodied practices also came into play when people brought their custom to these workplaces. Often, in bringing a broken or worn object to be mended, what these people were seeking to do was to maintain or re-establish a relationship between their bodies and their familiar, habitual things. We were witness to some profound examples of how subjectivities are linked to materialities. On one location, an older woman brought in a pair of slippers she'd bought at Woolworth's for a few pounds, because their soles had worn through. When informed that the repair would cost her £15 she agreed to the price. Her justification: "They are so comfortable". The blacksmith told us a story of a couple that came to him with a saucepan needing a new handle. When informed that it would be cheaper to buy a new one, they replied, "But it wouldn't make porridge like the old one". People have an "almost ritualistic connection to these objects", he commented.[14] The objects establish zones of comfort and identity; when the object ceases to function, this is threatened, and only the repairer can set things right again.

One more aspect of embodied practice worth mentioning here is the way the images triggered multi-sensory, and multi-temporal, responses in the people who interacted with them. A woman at the Bridport exhibition said, "I can smell my grandfather's workshop when I look at these photographs". Other people commented about the way the images triggered memories of tactile sensations, of other places and pasts. They wanted to share these memories, and

the exhibitions became spaces for quite intimate exchanges, often between strangers. There were animated conversations in front of the images on display, with people reminiscing and reflecting, but also talking about the objects in the images, how they were used, and then moving on to discussions about other things—lamenting the throwaway society and the decline of local shops, talking about their personal experience of cultural and economic change.

Return

We return to Benjamin, where we began: "The film, on the one hand, extends our comprehension of the necessities which rule our lives; on the other hand, it manages to assure us of an immense and unexpected field of action".[15] We have attempted here to share some of the "unexpected field of action" we explored during this project, a field where visual and material research methods were inextricably entangled. Our explorations with words and pictures involved a range of processes, technologies and embodied practices, some configurations of which we have sketched here. The work was complex, but incredibly rich—and unlike any other research project we've ever been involved with, partly because we allowed ourselves to be drawn into these places, and the people in them. The richness came in part too because we allowed ourselves to engage emotionally as well as intellectually, and not to censor our attention or to insist, always, on a critical stance in relation to the things we studied. We occupied a muddier, but perhaps more rewarding, middle ground. In mending, there is a distinction made between 'visible' and 'invisible' mending, depending on whether the mend exposes or conceals the evidence of repair. Our research was, essentially, a practice of visible mending, in which we made no attempt to hide the joins and seams, the stitches and solder.

References

1. W. Benjamin, 'The work of art in the age of mechanical reproduction', in *Illuminations* (London, Pimlico, 1999) 229-30.
2. J. Agee and W. Evans, *Let Us Now Praise Famous Men* (Boston, Houghton Mifflin, 1941) xv.
3. S. Pink, *Doing Sensory Ethnography* (London, Sage, 2009).
4. G. Rose and D. Tolia-Kelly, 'Visuality/materiality: introducing a manifesto for practice', in *Visuality/Materiality* (Farnham, Ashgate, 2012) 3.
5. Ibid.
6. G. Dyer, *The Ongoing Moment* (London, Little, Brown, 2005) 7.
7. Agee and Evans, 1941, xiv.
8. Interview with Jessica Rance, 21 February 2012.
9. C. DeSilvey and James R. Ryan, '21 Stories', *Cultural Geographies*, forthcoming.
10. Dorothea Lange, cited in M. Meltzer, *Dorothea Lange: A Photographer's Life*, (New York, Syracuse University Press, 2000) p.vii.
11. Benjamin, 1999, 230.
12. T. Dant, *Materiality and Society* (Maidenhead, Open University Press, 2004).
13. Interview with Nicholas Abrams, 1 June 2011.
14. Interview with Steve Willdig, 18 November 2010.
15. Benjamin, 1999, 229.